■SCHOLASTIC

Vocabulary Games
for Any Word List

JANE SULLIVAN & **MIDGE MADDEN**

New York • Toronto • London • Auckland • Sydney **Teaching**
Mexico City • New Delhi • Hong Kong • Buenos Aires *Resources*

To Grace, my niece, who will make a fine teacher.
—J.S.

To Braden, my inquisitive grandson. May you always
be intrigued by those big words you love.
— M.M

Pages 208–209, 222, 238–240 from *Teaching Phonics & Word Study in the Intermediate Grades: A Complete Source Book* © 2001 by Wiley Blevins. Reprinted with permission.

Editor: Sarah Longhi
Content editor: Carol Ghiglieri
Interior designer: Melinda Belter

ISBN-13: 978-0-545-10101-1
ISBN-10: 0-545-10101-8

Copyright © 2010 by Jane Sullivan and Midge Madden.
All rights reserved. Published by Scholastic Inc.
Printed in the U.S.A.

4 5 6 7 8 9 10   40   16 15 14 13 12

Contents

Introduction

In talking with today's middle school teachers, we often hear them express concern that students lack the reading fluency necessary for successful comprehension. One reason for this problem lies in the fact that texts in the middle and upper grades are simply more difficult: Sentences lengthen and become more complex, and authors use words that aren't typically part of students' speaking vocabulary. As a result, students can spend several seconds sounding out a word and/or puzzling over its meaning—a pause that creates a gap in the rhythm essential to comprehension. Consider this sentence from Conn Iggulden's *The Dangerous Book for Boys* (2007): "The easy vanish is simple to perform but very deceptive" (p. 192). The words *vanish, perform,* and *deceptive* are not words you often hear fourth, fifth, or sixth graders use. It's likely that students don't recognize them readily in print. They might make educated guesses for the meaning of the words *vanish* and *perform* using context but there are no clues for *deceptive*. Thus meaning is lost.

Teachers know that the solution lies in more vocabulary instruction. But how? What is the best approach? Beck, McKeown, and Lucan's analysis of research teaches us that students must have multiple encounters with a word before it becomes a meaningful part of their vocabulary (2002). Yet according to that research, there has been little progress in vocabulary instruction over the years. So, how do we engage students when the time comes for a lesson on vocabulary? In their research, Blachowicz, Fisher, and Ogle (2006) examine eight questions that they urge teachers to ask when planning vocabulary instruction. Among those questions, the following are pertinent to our discussion:

- What do we know about vocabulary knowledge?

- What do we know about good vocabulary instruction?

- What words should be taught?

- We both know from personal experience that these are questions teachers frequently ask.

What Do We Know About Vocabulary Knowledge and Instruction?

A great deal of research describes the strong link between vocabulary knowledge and reading comprehension. It's also true that a wide gap in verbal ability exists between economically advantaged and disadvantaged kindergartners, a gap that widens as these students progress through the grades. For these students, particularly, vocabulary instruction is essential to academic success. And while more is better, any instruction is better than none at all. If vocabulary instruction is essential to academic success and some instruction is better than none at all, we can no longer ignore the importance of teaching vocabulary. Yet, explicit teaching of vocabulary is too often overlooked in today's classrooms.

Perhaps many teachers remain uncertain about effective instructional strategies for teaching new words. Blachowicz, Fisher, and Ogle (2006) identify the elements that make up "good vocabulary instruction":

- An environment that fosters "word consciousness"
- Intentional teaching of select words and repeated exposure, use, and practice
- Teaching elements of words—e.g., roots, prefixes, suffixes
- Teaching use of reference works (such as encyclopedia or dictionaries)

While all of the above are essential, most critical to us is creating a word-conscious learning community. In classrooms where we see teachers and students engaged in word inquiry, wondering over nuances of meaning, we find readers who know and *use* sophisticated vocabulary.

What Words Should Be Taught?

Beck and her colleagues (2008) use the term "word tiers" to identify words that should be taught. They suggest that many of the words students encounter in texts can be divided into three tiers. Tier 1 words are the basic, familiar words heard every day (*go, lunch, very*). Words that fall into the Tier 2 category include those that readers encounter in written text but do not often hear or use in everyday conversation (*scurry, potential, empathetic*). Tier 3 words are those rare words not often encountered in texts *or* talk (*photosynthesize, coefficient, pilaster*). We agree with Beck and her colleagues who argue that teachers should intensively work with Tier 2 words in teaching vocabulary. These Tier 2 words are also the targeted words to use in the games we describe in this book.

The major thrust of this book is not *how to teach* new vocabulary. Many authors (Beck, 2002; Johnson, 2001; Allen, 1999) have covered that topic in great detail. We focus here on strategies that motivate students to engage fully in the repeated exposures, authentic use, and the practice needed for successful word learning.

But how do we teachers make this repeated practice enticing to students? One way is through play. The competition built into word games motivates students, holds their attention, and makes learning a wholly enjoyable activity. In this book we describe word games that we have used with classroom teachers and reading tutors to enliven vocabulary instruction for both proficient and struggling readers.

We have grouped the games according to their main purpose. Games that appear in Chapter 1, for example, provide practice in developing upper-grade sight vocabulary. In Chapter 2, we include games that focus on word structures (prefixes and suffixes) to teach word meanings. Chapter 3 contains synonym-based games that help students associate related words while expanding their word-choice capacity. In Chapter 4 we describe games that help students use context clues to understand word meanings and grasp common idiomatic expressions. Chapter 5 features review games that focus on combinations of word-learning strategies.

We also include suggestions for altering the games to better fit the purpose of the instruction. For example, while the game Word Sensation (Chapter 1) focuses on sight vocabulary, we include a modification should you wish to use the same format to emphasize the definitions of the words.

Today's teachers face classrooms of students whose afternoons are absorbed by such captivating activities as listening to iPods, surfing the Internet, and playing video games. These are our competition. Our challenge is to engage our students' attention, to build competition, motivation, and entertainment as well as learning into the hours these same students spend with us.

Helpful Word Lists to Consider

We believe that the best source for words used in these games is the text or texts students are currently reading. Drill and practice with vocabulary found in assigned or self-selected texts will enable students to read with the desirable fluency and comprehension that we, as teachers of reading, seek. Nevertheless, we have also included in the Appendix some word lists that you may find helpful in creating the word games listed in this book.

A well-known reference for sight words (i.e., words that occur frequently and should be recognized automatically or "on first sight" by readers) is the Dolch Word List. This list contains the 220 words most commonly found in reading texts (excluding nouns). Another word list frequently used for developing students' sight vocabulary is Fry's Instant Sight Word List. This is a list of 1,000 words that students need to know in order to develop a powerful sight vocabulary. (The first 300 words make up 65 percent of all written material contained in newspaper articles, magazines, textbooks, and children's stories and novels.) Both the Dolch and Fry lists can be found easily online.

You may also want to refer to "A List of Essential Words by Grade Level," compiled by Marzano, Kendall, and Paynter (http://www.docstoc.com/docs/ 2195050/Appendix-A-List-of-Essential-Words-by-Grade-Level). This list identifies a body of 6,768 basic words that appear frequently in academic texts and are few enough to have instructional value. The authors suggest that these words be taught to support the language development of students at risk and that instruction should focus only on words not already known.

Wiley Blevins's *Teaching Phonics & Word Study in the Intermediate Grades: A Complete Source Book* is an excellent source for other word lists. The text includes lists of words with double consonants, with similar consonant blends, or that fall into the same phonogram category (i.e., letter clusters that include the vowel and consonants that follow: *-ade* and *-ent* for example.) There are also lists of words that share similar prefixes, suffixes and language origin (Greek and Latin). For the convenience of teachers who plan to use the games we have described in this book, we have included several lists from Blevins's text on pages 73–79:

- Words that begin with the prefixes *un-* and *in-, im-, ir-, il-*)

- Words that end in the suffixes *-er, -est, -ful*

- Common synonyms

- Common antonyms

We hope you find these lists useful, but let us say again that we urge you to add to these lists from the reading vocabularies your students encounter in their reading, and to encourage your students to do the same.

—Jane Sullivan and Midge Madden

CHAPTER 1

DEVELOPING SIGHT VOCABULARY

We teachers of literacy recognize the important role vocabulary plays in our students' comprehension. We are also aware of the role "knowing the word on sight" plays in that task. Developing sight vocabulary is simpler in primary grades. The text we ask these students to read contains words typically present in a child's oral vocabulary. With repetition, he or she learns to recognize a word in print that's already known when it is spoken. In the middle grades, however, the task of word acquisition increases in difficulty. Students in the middle grades frequently encounter words they have heard spoken, but have never seen in print. They also come across high-utility words that are utterly foreign to them, in print as well as in speech. In both situations, learning generally takes place after seeing the word multiple times. A few students, however, will continue to stumble over words in text that they use easily in speech—and they will need more intensive support with sight word recognition.

Whether a word is new simply in print or new to both the ear and eye, all students benefit from the repetition that allows them to "own" a word in print. Thus, the focus of the games in this chapter is primarily on word recognition. We do, however, suggest modifications for each, so that reinforcement of the meaning of these words can also be included.

CHAPTER 1
GAMES

Word Sensation

Building a Mountain

Wic-Wac-Word

Word Sensation

This matching game is based on the familiar game Concentration. Easy to prepare, it gives students the opportunity to practice recognition of words that have not yet been firmly established in their sight vocabulary word bank.

VOCABULARY FOCUS Students strengthen sight vocabulary (and word meanings) by identifying pairs of words in isolation.

Object of This Game

To collect the most pairs of matching cards. (Claim one or more pair of word cards on each turn by correctly identifying and defining the word on the first card and finding the matching card.)

Materials

✔ Blank Cards template (page 74)

✔ Heavy paper or cardstock

✔ Word Sensation Record Sheet (page 12)

Number of Players

This game is designed for two players and a monitor. The monitor must know all the words as well as their definitions and may use the Word Sensation Record Sheet described in the preparation section below.

Preparation

1. Photocopy the word card template on heavy paper or cardstock.

2. Choose 6 to 12 challenging vocabulary words from the students' current reading.

3. Print each of the selected words on two word cards so that you have a deck of 12 (or up to 24) cards to use for the game (see illustration on following page).

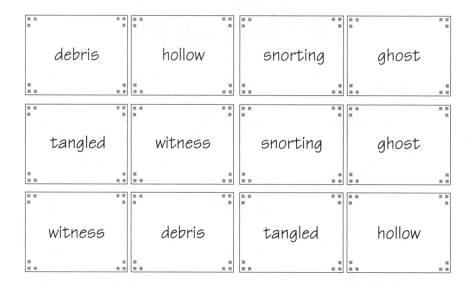

debris	hollow	snorting	ghost
tangled	witness	snorting	ghost
witness	debris	tangled	hollow

3. Fill in (or have students fill in) the Word Sensation Record Sheet that the monitor can refer to when necessary. The sheet should list each word in the deck along with a short definition (see the example below).

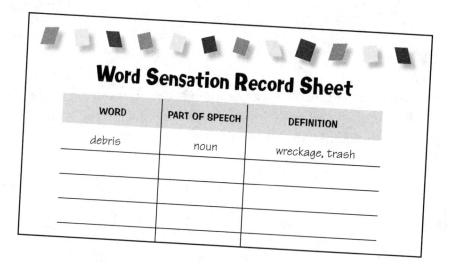

Word Sensation Record Sheet

WORD	PART OF SPEECH	DEFINITION
debris	noun	wreckage, trash

Directions for Playing

1. Shuffle the cards.

2. Lay the cards out facedown on a flat surface in rows and columns so that they form a rectangle.

3. Players take turns turning over two cards—one at a time.

4. The player reads the first card he or she has turned over. He or she must then define the word or use it correctly in a sentence. If the player hesitates or mispronounces the word, the monitor should step in and pronounce the word. The player then repeats the word.

Example:

Nate reaches for the first card. "Hmmm. And the word is deb-ris.*"*

Jane, acting as monitor, provides the correct pronunciation. "De-brée."

"Oh, right—de-brée," repeats Nate, adjusting his pronunciation.

"Can you say what that word means or use it in a sentence?" asks Jane.

"Sure," says Nate. "Mom told Joey to get his debris off the floor."

The monitor may also assist with a definition by a) providing a sentence with the word in context so the player can provide the definition, or b) by providing the definition and having the player think of a sentence with the word in context.

5. If the word on the first card matches the word on the second, the player keeps the pair and takes another turn.

6. If the cards do not match, the player repeats step 4 for the word on the second card turned over, then turns both cards back over, returning them to the same position.

7. Player 2 then takes a turn and follows the steps above.

8. When all cards have been paired, the player who has collected the most pairs is the winner.

Game Variations

To add more challenge, players can provide the following when they turn over a card:

- A synonym for the word

- An antonym for the word

- A prefix or suffix to create a new word

Word Sensation Record Sheet

WORD	PART OF SPEECH	DEFINITION

Building a Mountain

This game gives students practice in word recognition, focusing on words that they find particularly troublesome. In the game, the "mountain" that is built is the pile of known words, which gets higher over time as students master formerly troublesome words. You can begin an individual reading session with a student by playing a round of Building a Mountain. The game should not take more than five minutes.

VOCABULARY FOCUS

Provide a regular review of difficult or unfamiliar words, thus helping students strengthen the "instant recognition" required for reading fluency.

Object of This Game

To correctly identify difficult or unknown words on sight.

Materials

✔ Blank Cards template (page 74)

✔ Heavy paper or cardstock

Number of Players

This game is played by one student, with the assistance of a teacher or an aide.

Preparation

1. Photocopy the word card reproducible on heavy paper or cardstock.

2. Select at least ten words that are not yet in the student's sight vocabulary and print each one on a separate card. On the opposite side of the cards, provide a short sentence, phrase, or illustration to serve as a clue to the word's meaning.

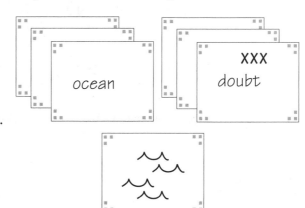

Directions for Playing

1. Stack the prepared word cards in a deck.

2. Lay a card in front of the student, word-side up, and ask him or her to pronounce the word. If the student identifies the word correctly without hesitation (a very brief pause is acceptable), place a small check mark in the corner of the card.

3. If the student hesitates too long or cannot identify the word, turn the card over and allow him or her to look at the illustration or read the sentence or phrase aloud. If the student still cannot recognize the word, pronounce it yourself. In either case, the card does not receive a check.

4. When a word card has three check marks on it, move the word from the working deck to the "mountain" deck, which will grow over time. As the working deck shrinks, add more words to it to keep the game going and student's vocabulary expanding. The game should be played at each individual reading session.

NOTE

The first time the student plays the game, you will have only one deck of cards—the "working deck." Over time, a second deck, the "mountain" deck, will be created, and you can add new word cards to the working deck.

Game Variations

1. The game can be played with two or three players. Each player can take a turn at identifying the word.

2. The player is required to not only identify the word but to give its definition (or use it in a sentence) as well.

3. Students can prepare game cards to challenge classmates.

Wic-Wac-Word

Offering a fun twist on Tic-Tac-Toe, this game provides practice in word recognition as student pairs vie to be the first to claim three boxes on the grid, running down, across, or diagonally.

VOCABULARY FOCUS Practice identifying words that are new or challenging, to increase sight-word mastery.

Object of This Game

To be the first to correctly identify three words on the game grid, running down, across, or on the diagonal.

Number of Players

This game is designed for two players.

Preparation

1. Photocopy a blank Wic-Wac-Word grid for each pair of players.

2. Select nine words that both players need practice identifying. In each of the nine boxes, print one of the pair's target words.

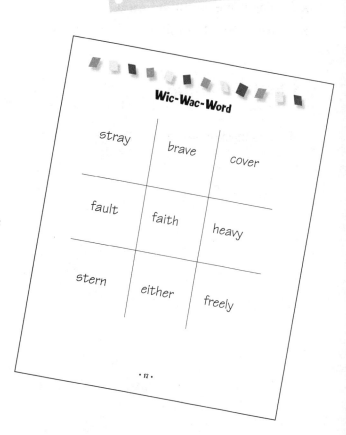

Materials

✔ Wic-Wac-Word grid (page 17)

✔ Heavy paper or cardstock (optional; see note on the following page)

✔ Water-based pen

Directions for Playing

1. Players flip a coin to decide who will go first.

2. The first player chooses whether he or she will be X or O. The player then selects a word in one of the boxes and says it out loud. If the player says the word correctly, he or she writes an X or O in that box.

3. If the player cannot pronounce the word correctly, he or she cannot claim the box.

4. The second player now takes a turn.

5. The game continues until one of the players succeeds in "claiming" three boxes running down, across, or on the diagonal.

Game Variation

Players must provide a definition for the word in addition to identifying it.

Wic-Wac-Word

WORDS THAT GROW
Roots and Affixes

One way we can play with words is to "make them grow." Consider the word *work*, for example. We can make that word grow by adding a prefix: *re*work. We can also add any number of suffixes—for instance, work*able*, work*ing*, and work*er*. When we capture the root, *work*, and recognize the meaning of the prefix or suffix, the meaning of these words becomes clear: *work again*, *able to work*, and so on.

The games in this chapter provide practice in assembling and disassembling words with common prefixes and suffixes. Before embarking on these games, we must first select prefixes and suffixes and teach their pronunciation and meaning. We also need to teach students the crucial role such prefixes or suffixes play, namely that they change the part of speech. So, for example, the suffix *-ly* changes the adjectives *late* and *slow* into the adverbs *lately* and *slowly*. Once the concept is taught, students need to apply it—and the games in this chapter give them practice in doing so. Here are a couple of points to keep in mind:

- Choose words from the students' reading. Better yet, let students find the words themselves. They can be active participants in creating the game cards as well as playing with them.

- These games are designed to give the necessary exposure to the selected words so that students will, in time, automatically associate the word with its meaning. Lessons that teach strategies for learning definitions of the words should always precede the playing of the games.

CHAPTER 2
GAMES

Digging for Roots

Dictionary Search

Pick-a-Prefix

Digging for Roots

Digging for Roots is similar to the well-loved card game Go Fish. In this game, however, the sets of cards students will be seeking are not aces or jacks but root words and their derivatives (a "derivative" is a longer word that contains the root word within it—for example, *atomic* is a derivative of *atom*).

VOCABULARY FOCUS   Practice the key skill of identifying roots and their derivatives.

Object of This Game

To collect the most sets of cards. (A complete "set" consists of three cards— the root and two derivatives.)

Materials

✔ Digging for Roots Cards template (page 22)

✔ Heavy paper or cardstock

Number of Players

This game is designed for three to five players.

Preparation

1. Photocopy the word card reproducible onto heavy paper or cardstock.

2. Prepare at least ten complete sets of cards. (The number of sets can vary, depending on the number and skill level of the players.) Each set should contain one root word and two derivatives. For example, if one card contains the root word *work*, the other two cards that would complete the set might be *rework* and *workable*.

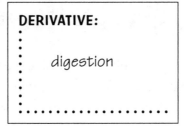

ROOT:

digest

DERIVATIVE:

digestion

DERIVATIVE:

digestive

Directions for Playing

1. The dealer shuffles the deck and deals five cards to each player.

2. The remaining cards are placed in a pile where all players can reach them.

3. The player to the right of the dealer begins. He or she turns to one of the other players and asks that player to give up all cards containing a specified root. The "asker" must be in possession of either the root or one of the derivatives, and both roots and derivatives must be handed over when asked for.

    ### Example:

    Pam: Quentin, give me all your cards that contain the root press.

4. If the player who's been asked is holding any of the cards in the set (either the root or derivatives), he or she must hand them all over, and the asker takes another turn. If this player does *not* have any cards in the set, the asker draws a card from the deck. If he or she draws a card that belongs to the set in question, he or she gets to take another turn. If the card drawn is not a match, the turn ends, and the player to the right takes a turn. (Remind younger students to keep their ears open to find out who might have cards they need to complete their sets.)

5. Play continues. When a player forms a complete set, he or she lays it down and reads the words on the cards. If a player cannot read one or more words in the set, he or she cannot count that set in the final tally. The game ends when all sets have been collected. The winner is the player with the most sets.

Game Variations

1. The derivatives may all have the same suffix and/or prefix.

2. The root word as well as the two derivatives can be written on all three cards in the set.

3. Players may each have a Root Word/Derivatives list (see sample list below).

4. For younger players, underline the root within each derivative on word cards.

Root Words and Derivatives

digest	digestion	digestive
dentist	dental	dentistry
faith	faithful	faithless
victor	victory	victorious
study	student	studious
child	childish	childhood
brave	bravery	bravest
consider	considerable	consideration
collect	collective	collection
free	freely	freedom
animate	inanimate	animation
danger	endanger	dangerous
fire	firecracker	firefly
air	airline	airplane
require	required	requirement
temper	temperament	temperamental
bump	bumper	bumpy
care	carefree	careless
civil	civilized	civilization
differ	difference	different
approve	disapprove	disapproval
like	dislike	likable
slave	enslave	slavery
fool	foolish	foolproof
repeat	repetition	repetitious

Digging for Roots Cards

ROOT:

ROOT:

DERIVATIVE:

DERIVATIVE:

DERIVATIVE:

DERIVATIVE:

Dictionary Search

In *Creating Robust Vocabulary* (2008), Isabel Beck, Margaret McKeown, and Linda Kucan point out that after the introduction of a new word and its definition, robust vocabulary instruction requires frequent encounters with the word—in and out of context. This game addresses that need. The task in Dictionary Search is not so much to "recall" the definition of a word, but to recognize it, given several choices. This, as experts point out, is an easier task. As with the other games in this book, the words used here as examples are just that: *examples*. The way for your students to get the greatest benefit from all the games in this book is to choose words directly from their reading.

> **VOCABULARY FOCUS** Strengthen vocabulary and reinforce students' knowledge of parts of speech and common suffixes.

Object of This Game

To choose the correct definition of a word containing a suffix from among three choices.

Materials

✔ Dictionary Search Cards template (page 26)

✔ Dictionaries

Number of Players

This game is designed for two teams, each with three or four players.

NOTE

Be sure to choose a dictionary that students can use easily—Isabel Beck and her colleagues cite Collins COBUILD English Language Dictionary *as one that "provides discursive explanations rather than traditional definitions" (Beck, McKeown, & Kucan, 2002, p. 123). Other dictionaries such as* Scholastic Children's Dictionary, The DK Children's Illustrated Dictionary, *or* Webster's New World Children's Dictionary *are good references.*

Preparation

1. Select at least ten words from students' reading that contain suffixes (or have students identify the words themselves).

2. Follow these directions (or have teams follow them) to prepare a game card for each word:

   • First write a sentence using the word.

   • Then, write a sentence stem that asks for the definition of the word.

   • Include three possible choices, one correct and two incorrect (see examples below).

SENTENCE

Jake was late for soccer practice and walked briskly to the field.

_____ Briskly _____ is a (an) _____ adverb _____

that means . . .

1. slow
2. fast
3. without care

SENTENCE

Marta makes the wisest choices after taking a deep breath and thinking carefully.

_____ Wisest _____ is a (an) _____ adjective _____

that means . . .

1. best
2. smartest
3. first

Directions for Playing

1. The two teams take turns reading the word cards and asking the opposing team to select the correct definition for the target word.

2. A member from the opposing team reads the item aloud, along with the three possible choices.

3. Team members may consult with each other, but time should be limited (from ten seconds to one minute, depending on age and skill level of students).

4. Teams earn points for each correct response. The team with the most points at the end of play wins.

Game Variations

1. Prepare the definitions ahead of time, rather than having students construct the list.

2. Number of players can vary from two individuals to two teams that include everyone in the class—depending on age and expertise.

3. Vary the number of distracters on each card.

4. Play the game with other challenging vocabulary words.

Dictionary Search Cards

SENTENCE

_____

_____

_____ is a (an) _____

that means . . .

1. _____

2. _____

3. _____

SENTENCE

_____

_____

_____ is a (an) _____

that means . . .

1. _____

2. _____

3. _____

Pick-a-Prefix

Researchers have identified 11 common prefixes that students come across in their reading, beginning in third grade: *un-, e-, in-, im-* (meaning "not"), *ir-, dis-, en-, em-, non-, im-* (meaning "in or "into"), *over-,* and *mis-.* Knowing these prefixes will greatly enhance students' ability to figure out the meaning of unfamiliar words when they encounter them in their reading. In this game, student teams are given a specific prefix and must then come up with words containing that prefix, as well as their definitions. In addition to giving students practice learning prefixes, the game also gives them an opportunity to distinguish between actual prefixes and instances when those same letters do not function as prefixes (*inhabit* versus *interest,* for example).

VOCABULARY
FOCUS

Students review their knowledge of prefixes and words that contain them.

Object of This Game

Come up with the most words (along with their definitions) that feature the target prefix.

Materials

✔ Pick-a-Prefix Record Sheet (page 29)

✔ Dictionaries

Number of Players

This game is designed for two or more teams, each with two to four players.

NOTE

When there are more than two players per team, one team member should be designated the "captain" who will create a single list compiled from all team members.

Preparation

1. Select a prefix that students will use to play the game.

2. You may wish to compile a list of words that begin with the designated prefix, to serve as a reference sheet (see example below).

PREFIX	MEANING	EXAMPLES
ambi-	both	ambidextrous, ambiguous, ambivalent
anti-	against	antifreeze, anti-war, antidote, antiseptic
bene-	good	benefactor, benefit, benediction, beneficial
bi-	two	bicycle, bicameral, bimonthly, biceps
circum-	around	circumnavigate, circumference, circumvent
deca-	ten	decade, decathlon, decameter
ex-	out of	exfoliate, exhale, exhaust, exempt
fore-	ahead of	forecast, forearm, foretell, foreground
im-, in-	in, into	incubate, immigrate, inborn, incursion
mono-	one	monologue, monoplane, monopoly
mal-	bad	malpractice, malignant, malice, malign

Directions for Playing

1. Assign the target prefix.

2. Give teams a set amount of time (this will depend on the age and skill level of your students). Have them work independently to list as many words as they can with the prefix, along with their definitions. They may *not* use dictionaries or other reference materials.

3. When time is called, allow members of each team to share their lists and compile a master list. If any definitions are disputed by an opposing team, a dictionary can be consulted.

4. The team that has compiled the longest list of words, along with appropriate definitions, is the winner.

Game Variation

Students can play one-on-one, or even individually, for more prefix practice.

Pick-a-Prefix Record Sheet

INSTRUCTIONS: Think of as many words featuring the target prefix as you can. Then write their definitions WITHOUT checking a dictionary.

TARGET PREFIX

WORDS	DEFINITIONS

CHAPTER 3

SYNONYMS

How often have we teachers heard our students ask, "What's another word for . . . ?" Most of our learners would benefit enormously by "freshening" their vocabularies, incorporating words that mean the same or almost the same thing, thus allowing them to avoid the "same old same old" in their speech and writing. Worth considering when we reflect on how to encourage students to learn replacements for such "tired words" is what John O. E. Clark (1988) advises in the preface to *Word for Word: A Dictionary of Synonyms:* "Synonyms are seldom exact, but can provide variety to relieve what would otherwise be a limited and ultimately boring vocabulary." We agree.

The games in this chapter are designed to do more than simply increase students' vocabularies. They also stimulate an overall word awareness. Our students need to study words in terms of their subtle differences. So, before you introduce these games, we urge you to hold discussions on the nuances that separate synonyms. It's important for students to understand that synonyms are not "twins." There are slight differences between nearly all such words. Take *dam* and *barricade,* for example. While we know that a dam is a type of barricade, we can think of other words that fall into that category as well, yet which describe something somewhat different: *roadblock* or *fort,* for example. Discussing these kinds of distinctions extends our students' word awareness. Studying synonyms of words encourages the depth of knowledge that, in addition to enhancing students' reading skills, will also improve their writing.

CHAPTER 3
GAMES

What's the Word?

R-E-A-D-O

Wheel of Words

What's the Word?

What's the Word? is a fun way to help students build their reading vocabularies. Before playing, make sure students understand that a word's *synonym* is another word that means almost the same thing. For example, *quiet* is a synonym for *silent*; *clean* is a synonym for *spotless*.

VOCABULARY FOCUS Students bolster their vocabularies by correctly identifying synonyms for known words.

Object of This Game

To supply synonyms for target words.

Number of Players

This game is designed for three or more players, with one student serving as referee (the teacher may play this role).

Materials

- ✔ What's the Word? Cards template (page 34)
- ✔ Heavy paper or cardstock
- ✔ Dictionary or thesaurus (optional)

NOTE

If more than three players are participating, organize the group into two opposing teams. In addition, one student should serve as the judge who will decide whether the answer is acceptable if and when a dispute arises (the teacher may play this role).

Preparation

1. Photocopy the What's the Word? Cards template onto heavy paper or cardstock.

2. Prepare a deck of cards (15–20 cards, depending on the age and skill level of students) that contain challenging words students have recently encountered in their reading. On each card, print the word, its part of speech, and a sentence containing that word.

Example

silent . . . adjective . . . The whole class was *silent during the announcement.*

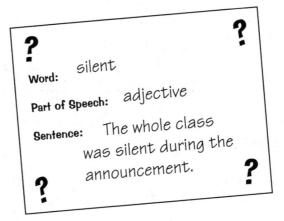

Directions for Playing

1. The first player (or team member) draws a card from the deck and reads the word, the part of speech, and the sentence.

2. The opposing player (or team member) provides a synonym for the word that makes sense in the sentence.

3. If the player is correct, he or she (or the team) receives a point. Then steps 1 and 2 are repeated. (If teams are playing, another member of the team now takes a turn.)

4. If, on the other hand, the player misses, the two players (or teams) switch roles.

5. If a dispute arises, the individual appointed judge decides whether the answer is acceptable or not. (A dictionary or thesaurus can be consulted if needed.)

6. At the end of the game, the player (or team) that has earned the most points wins the game.

Game Variations

■ Have students work in teams to prepare the cards themselves.

■ In addition to the target word, a choice of possible synonyms may be included on the card.

■ A circle of players may play individually, each taking a turn in order.

What's the Word? Cards

? ?	? ?
Word: Part of Speech: Sentence: ? ?	Word: Part of Speech: Sentence: ? ?
? ? Word: Part of Speech: Sentence: ? ?	? ? Word: Part of Speech: Sentence: ? ?
? ? Word: Part of Speech: Sentence: ? ?	? ? Word: Part of Speech: Sentence: ? ?

R-E-A-D-O

Based on the game Bingo, our version, R-E-A-D-O, provides excellent practice matching vocabulary words to their meanings so that students can "own" the words—that is, recognize their meaning instantly when they encounter them in their reading.

VOCABULARY
FOCUS

Students practice selecting a synonym for target words.

Object of This Game

To be the first to get "R-E-A-D-O," five squares on their game card, running down, across, or diagonally. (With the help of context clues, students match new vocabulary with their synonyms on their game cards.)

✔ R-E-A-D-O game card template (page 38)

✔ R-E-A-D-O Caller Cards template (page 39)

✔ Beans or buttons (or other small items) to serve as markers

✔ Water-based pens (optional)

Number of Players

This game is designed for any number of players, from two students to the entire class.

Preparation

1. Photocopy the R-E-A-D-O game card template onto cardstock to create game cards. Laminate if desired.

2. Photocopy the caller card template on cardstock. These can also be laminated for repeated use.

3. To prepare the caller cards, follow these directions:

   • Assign at least five vocabulary words to each of the five columns on the game card (R, E, A, D, or O).

- For each word, print a synonym of the word on one of the cards. For example, if one of your vocabulary words is *select*, you might write *choose* on one of the caller cards. Be sure to pick a synonym students will know.

- On that same card, also write a sentence, using the synonym— for example, *I like to choose my own books.*

- Lastly, print the target word in the Answer space.

R E A D O

Synonym: choose

Sentence: I like to choose my own books.

Answer: select

R E A D O

Synonym: cold

Sentence: In the mornings, the mountain air was cold.

Answer: frigid

4. To prepare game cards, follow these directions:

- Write the selected vocabulary words on the board. You must have at least 24 words, one for each square on the card, excluding the free space.

- Distribute a blank game card to each player.

- Instruct students to fill in the boxes by randomly filling the squares with the vocabulary words, one word per box. If cards are laminated, give students water-based pens to write in the words.

Directions for Playing

1. Select one student to be caller (the teacher can also fill this role).

2. Have players get their game cards ready, and provide them with markers.

3. Tell players to put a marker on their free space.

4. The caller chooses a card from the pile and reads the synonym aloud, assigning it to one of the lettered columns.
   For example: "R: choose" or "E: cold." The caller then reads the sentence on the card. After reading each card, the caller puts it aside.

NOTE

> *It's up to the caller to keep track of each card, and to remember if it was assigned the letter R, E, A, D, or O. He or she can jot this on a sheet of paper or stack the cards in separate piles. This is important because the caller must verify that the person who calls out "Reado!" is in fact the winner.*

5. Players locate the target word and, if it appears in the correct column, cover the word with a marker.

6. When players have marked five squares in a row, either down, across, or on the diagonal, he or she shouts "READO!" The player calls out his or her words and the caller verifies that the words are correct. If so, the players has won the game.

7. If desired, the winner can become the caller of the next round.

Game Variations

1. The first letter of the target word can be given as well as its synonym.

2. The game can also be used to strengthen students' sight vocabulary. In that case, words on the caller cards should be the same as words on the game card.

3. Players can work in pairs to find and cover the correct word.

4. As each word is called, a player can volunteer and, when called on, respond by naming the target word aloud.

R	E	A	D	O
		FREE		

R-E-A-D-O Caller Cards

R E A D O

Synonym:

Sentence:

Answer:

R E A D O

Synonym:

Sentence:

Answer:

R E A D O

Synonym:

Sentence:

Answer:

R E A D O

Synonym:

Sentence:

Answer:

R E A D O

Synonym:

Sentence:

Answer:

R E A D O

Synonym:

Sentence:

Answer:

Wheel of Words

By teaching our students word meanings, we hope to encourage them to incorporate new words into their writing, as well as to recognize these word meanings when they read. To do this, they need to learn not only the definition of a word but its spelling as well. Wheel of Words requires players to hone their spelling skills as well as to glean meaning from context. Use this game to playfully practice one or two vocabulary words or a whole list.

VOCABULARY FOCUS
Students practice identifying and spelling target words based on context clues.

Object of This Game

To use a word clue and spelling skills to correctly guess a hidden word before opponents do.

Number of Players

This game is designed for three to five players, with one player serving as the "reader."

Preparation

1. Photocopy the Wheel of Words template and scorecard on cardstock and laminate.

2. Photocopy enough word cards to allow for the number of words you wish to review.

3. Prepare a set of word cards by printing the following: a clue to the target word, its part of speech, and its number of letters. The clue should be a sentence containing a synonym of the target word. The word itself, for the reader's information alone, should also be on the card.

Materials

✔ Wheel of Words template (page 43)

✔ Wheel of Words Scorecard (page 44)

✔ Wheel of Words Cards template (page 45)

✔ Heavy cardstock

✔ Scissors

✔ Paper clip and pencil to form a spinner

✔ Water-based pens

Sentence Clue: _She will search through her closet to try to find the costume._

Part of Speech: _verb_

Number of Letters: _7_

(Secret Word: _rummage_)

Directions for Playing

1. One student is chosen to be the reader. To begin, the reader chooses a word card. This contains the word players will try to guess. Only the reader sees the card.

2. The reader counts out the number of letters in the word and with a water-based pen, puts an X through any extra boxes at the bottom of the wheel template.

   For example, if the word is *rummage*, the reader crosses out three boxes, leaving seven blank, since *rummage* has seven letters, as shown below.

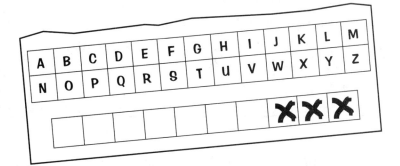

3. Next, the reader tells players the part of speech and reads the clue, a sentence that contains a synonym of the target word. The reader reads the sentence twice, the second time omitting the target word. Here's an example for the word *rummage*:

   *The Reader: "The word is a verb: She will **search** through her closet to try to find the costume. She will **blank** through her closet to try to find the costume."*

4. The first player spins the paper clip on the Wheel of Words spinner (see illustration) to determine how many points he or she will earn for guessing a letter correctly.

5. The player guesses a consonant (see note below about buying vowels). If the consonant is in the word, the reader uses a water-based pen to write that letter in the appropriate box (or boxes) and crosses out that letter in the alphabet list. The reader notes the player's points on the scorecard.

6. The player then takes another turn.

7. If the letter is not in the word, the player loses the points indicated in his spin. The next player takes a turn spinning the paper clip.

NOTE

During their turn, players can spend five points to "buy a vowel." For example, a player can "buy" the letter e. The reader then crosses out the letter in the alphabet list and fills it in the appropriate squares, if any. If there are no e's in the word, the player loses the five points but suffers no other penalty. Play continues.

8. At any time during a turn, a player can guess at the word. If the player guesses correctly, he or she keeps all the points earned. If the player's guess is incorrect, the turn is over and the player does not earn any points during that turn.

9. Once the word has been guessed correctly, the next player takes a turn and the procedure is repeated with a new word.

10. At the end of the game, the player with the most points wins the game.

Game Variations

1. Players may work in pairs to solve the puzzle.

2. Have students prepare the game cards.

Wheel of Words

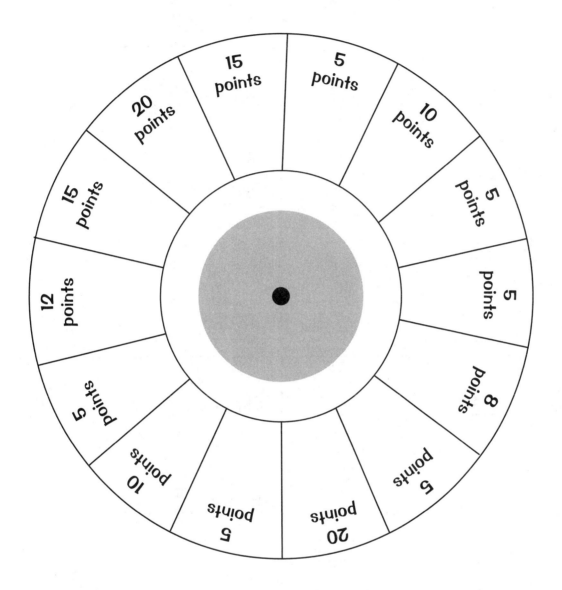

A	B	C	D	E	F	G	H	I	J	K	L	M
N	O	P	Q	R	S	T	U	V	W	X	Y	Z

Wheel of Words Scorecard

Player 1: _____

Points:

Player 2: _____

Points:

Player 3: _____

Points:

Player 4: _____

Points:

Wheel of Words Cards

Card 1

Sentence Clue: _____

_____

_____.

Part of Speech: _____

Number of Letters: _____

(Secret Word: _____)

Card 2

Sentence Clue: _____

_____

_____.

Part of Speech: _____

Number of Letters: _____

(Secret Word: _____)

Card 3

Sentence Clue: _____

_____

_____.

Part of Speech: _____

Number of Letters: _____

(Secret Word: _____)

Card 4

Sentence Clue: _____

_____

_____.

Part of Speech: _____

Number of Letters: _____

(Secret Word: _____)

CLUES IN CONTEXT

When using a word or phrase that might be unfamiliar to their readers, authors generally include the meaning, either directly or by providing clues so that meaning won't be lost. They can go about this in a number of different ways. Sometimes they insert a definition immediately after the word or phrase in question: *The aurora borealis, or northern lights, often appear in the sky above Alaska.* Sometimes the author includes a phrase in the text that hints at the meaning:

"Jane didn't appreciate my gift," I complained to my friend.
"Well, you shouldn't cast pearls before swine," she reminded me.

We know from the friend's response that casting pearls before swine is linked to "didn't appreciate." So, as readers, we get a notion of the meaning of that idiomatic expression.

We want to teach our students to look for such clues when they read. Giving them practice in this skill enables them to increase their vocabulary. It is also likely to improve their comprehension, since many readers simply skip over words whose meaning they don't know, thereby losing a piece of the text's meaning. The games we have included in this chapter provide students with practice in defining words in context.

CHAPTER 4
GAMES

Scavenger Hunt

Right or Wrong?

What's in an Idiom?

Scavenger Hunt

In this game, students search books, newspapers, or magazines for examples of words whose meanings are explained, or at least, hinted at, through examples or the use of synonyms.

VOCABULARY FOCUS Students practice using context clues to "guesstimate" the definition of a word not already in their vocabulary.

Object of This Game

To locate target words defined in context.

Number of Players

This game is designed to be played by teams of four or five members each.

Materials

✔ A variety of print materials, such as books, newspapers, and magazines

✔ Sticky notes

✔ Scratch paper

Preparation

1. Gather a variety of print materials that contain examples of words defined in context. Highlight the area on the page where each target word is located.

2. For each text, include a sticky note that lists the page numbers on which students will find target words that are defined in context.

Example:

National Geographic, August, 2007, page 12.

On that page, students will find the word *spontaneous* defined in context: *The biggest difference is that in war, everything is spontaneous. In the White House, everything is controlled.*

Students should recognize that in these two sentences, two opposite words are used. If you know the meaning of *controlled*, you can surmise the meaning of *spontaneous*.

Directions for Playing

1. Divide the class into teams of players.

2. Distribute materials to teams.

3. Give teams a set time in which to locate their words. The allotted time will vary, depending on the age and skill level of your students.

4. Team members can work together to locate the defined words, using the materials provided.

5. Once the unknown word is found, students use the clues provided in the text to define the word. Have them record the word and its meaning on a piece of scratch paper.

6. When time is called, the captain of each team of students shares with the class the words the team found, the definitions they arrived at and the type of clue that led them to that definition.

7. The team that finds the greatest number of words, defined correctly, is the winner.

Game Variation

If students need more assistance, you might also list the key word next to the reference source in the list:

National Geographic, August, 2007, page 12: spontaneous

Right or Wrong?

In answer to the question "What does this word mean?" we often respond by asking, "How is it used in the sentence?" Right or Wrong? gives students practice in the important skill of inferring a word's meaning.

VOCABULARY FOCUS Students practice using context to discern the meaning of new vocabulary.

Object of This Game:

To decide if the target word is used correctly or incorrectly in a sentence.

Materials

✔ Right or Wrong? Cards template (page 51)

✔ Heavy paper or cardstock

Number of Players

This game is designed for two players.

Preparation

1. Photocopy the Right or Wrong? word cards onto heavy paper or cardstock.

2. Compile a list of 10–20 newly introduced vocabulary words (you may also choose words students have had difficulty recognizing in reading).

3. For each word, write one or two sentences on a word card, placing the word in context. (You may need to provide two sentences to fully establish context.) For some of the words, use the word correctly in the context. For others, use the word inappropriately. You may also want to note whether each example is "right" or "wrong."

RIGHT OR WRONG?

Word: quarrelsome

Context: I really like Margaret. She is so quarrelsome.

(wrong)

RIGHT OR WRONG?

Word: scowled

Context: Annoyed by the noise in the classroom, the teacher scowled at the students.

(right)

Directions for Playing

1. Players flip a coin to decide who goes first. The first player draws a card from the top of the deck and reads the word on the card, followed by the sentence or sentences.

2. The second player must decide if the word in question has been used correctly in the sentence. If the word fits the context, he or she says that yes, the context is appropriate. (If the game is played in teams, team members can consult with each other. The time should be limited, however—20 or 30 seconds would be a reasonable amount of time.)

3. If the word is used incorrectly, the player must make an appropriate change so the word is then used correctly.

Example:

Elena draws a card and reads it: "Quarrelsome: I really like Margaret. She is so quarrelsome."

Chris: "No, that's wrong. I'll change it to: I really don't *like Margaret. She is so quarrelsome."*

If the responding player answers correctly, he or she "wins" the card. The roles then switch and the "caller" becomes the "responder." (If teams of players are playing, members should take turns.)

4. When all cards have been used, the player having the most cards is declared the winner.

Game Variations

1. Have students play in two teams of three or four players.

2. For large-group play, have students sit in a circle, each taking a turn in order.

3. For a simpler variation, players need only decide if the word is or is not used correctly, without correcting the sentence.

Right or Wrong? Cards

RIGHT OR WRONG?

Word:

Context:

RIGHT OR WRONG?

Word:

Context:

RIGHT OR WRONG?

Word:

Context:

RIGHT OR WRONG?

Word:

Context:

RIGHT OR WRONG?

Word:

Context:

RIGHT OR WRONG?

Word:

Context:

What's in an Idiom?

The *American Heritage Dictionary* defines *idiom* as follows:

> A speech form or an expression of a given language that is peculiar to itself grammatically or cannot be understood from the individual meanings of its elements, as in "keep tabs on."

Because idioms contain expressions that are unusual or whose meanings are different from what the individual elements would suggest, students—particularly second-language learners—often miss the author's meaning when he or she uses an idiom that students aren't familiar with.

The most important thing for our students to realize is that idioms are not meant to be taken literally. When a friend announces, "I have a frog in my throat," she does not mean that a green amphibian is living above her esophagus! Nor do we interpret her statement that way. Such a phrase is simply a colorful way of expressing the fact that her voice is hoarse. When listeners or readers understand the non-literal meaning of such phrases, then the speaker/writer and listener/reader have successfully communicated. Without this understanding, confusion results. This is why we need to acquaint our students with the common idioms they might encounter in their reading. What's in an Idiom? will give students exposure to common idioms.

VOCABULARY FOCUS

Strengthen students' knowledge of common idioms and their meanings.

Object of This Game

To match the most idioms with their meanings.

Number of Players

This game is designed for three to five players, with one student serving as dealer.

Materials

- ✔ What's in an Idiom? Cards template (page 55)
- ✔ What's in an Idiom? Record Sheet (page 56)
- ✔ Idiom List and Meanings (page 57)
- ✔ Markers or stickers in two different colors

Preparation

1. Refer to the list of idioms or collect examples of idioms from students' reading materials—or challenge student to think of some—and create pairs of idiom cards. For each pair, first write the idiom in a sentence. Then on a second card, "translate" the idiom, providing the meaning in simple English. For example, in the sample idiom pair shown below, the idiom card says *They pulled the wool over her eyes*, while the companion card gives the same meaning in plain language: *They fooled her.*

Idiom in a Sentence:

They pulled the wool over her eyes.

Meaning:

They fooled her.

NOTE

Depending on the skill level of your students, you may want to provide more context clues in your idiom card sentences.

2. When you've finished, you will have two decks of cards, one of idioms presented in sentences, and one of their meanings. Mark the back of cards in the idiom deck with one color and the back of the companion cards with a different color. You can also mark the face of each card in a deck with the same color, making it easier to keep the cards in the same deck together.

3. Complete the What's in an Idiom? Record Sheet based on the card sets you've created (or have students do this step). The dealer can refer to this sheet during play.

Directions for Playing

1. The dealer lays out five cards from the idiom deck, faceup in front of the players. He or she then deals each player five cards from the companion deck.

2. The first player compares his or her cards with the idiom cards displayed to see if he or she has a match. If the player's cards do not match any of the idioms, he or she can exchange *up to three* cards and get new ones. The player gives his or her cards to the dealer, who puts them at the bottom of the deck. The dealer then deals the player the same number of new cards from the top of the deck.

3. If the player can now make a match, he or she picks up the idiom card and reads both cards aloud. The dealer verifies that the match is correct. (If the dealer isn't sure, he or she can consult the record sheet.) The player's turn continues until he or she can make no more matches.

4. If the player has made a wrong match, he or she loses a turn and the player to the left takes a turn. The next player then takes a turn and the sequence is repeated.

5. The game is over when all cards have been matched.

6. When all cards have been matched, players count their pairs. The player having the most pairs of cards wins the game.

Game Variations

1. To make the game more interesting, make duplicates of some of the pairs.

2. Switch the decks so that players have the idioms in their hands while the partner cards with the meanings are laid out.

What's in an Idiom? Cards

Idiom in a Sentence:

Meaning:

Idiom in a Sentence:

Meaning:

Idiom in a Sentence:

Meaning:

What's in an Idiom? Record Sheet

IDIOM   MEANING

_____   _____

_____   _____

_____   _____

_____   _____

_____   _____

_____   _____

_____   _____

_____   _____

_____   _____

_____   _____

_____   _____

_____   _____

_____   _____

_____   _____

_____   _____

Idiom List and Meanings

IDIOMS IN SENTENCES	MEANINGS
They pulled the wool over her eyes.	They fooled her.
Keep your fingers crossed this is right.	Hope this is right.
He's a good egg.	He's a good person.
She hadn't seen hide nor hair of him.	She hadn't seen him at all.
She bought a pig in a poke.	She bought something without seeing it.
A computer costs an arm and a leg.	A computer costs a lot of money.
He cried wolf when he fell.	He pretended to need help when he fell.
I need to catch my breath.	I need to rest.
Their star player had feet of clay.	Their star player had faults.
I have a bone to pick with him.	I need to argue with him about that.
The race ended in a dead heat.	The race ended in a tie.
She forgot, so I jogged her memory.	She forgot, so I reminded her.
We got a green light on the project.	They said we could do our project.
I wasn't sure, so I took a shot in the dark.	I wasn't sure so I guessed.
Sarah shed light on the puzzle.	Sarah helped us understand the puzzle.
The room was spick-and-span.	The room was neat and clean.
I had to cool my heels while Joe ate.	I had to wait while Joe ate.
My dad is a dyed-in-the-wool Democrat.	My dad is an unchangeable Democrat.
Nate doesn't know beans about that.	Nate doesn't know anything about that.
He almost dove, but he got cold feet.	He almost dove, but he got scared.
Today is a red-letter day in my life.	Today is a memorable day in my life.
We will do it by hook or by crook.	We will do it one way or another.
I wore my best bib and tucker.	I wore my best clothes.
We were quiet until Mary broke the ice.	We were quiet until Mary made us comfortable by beginning to talk.

CHAPTER 5

COMBINED-SKILLS GAMES

The games in this chapter are more involved and call for strategy that will readily hold the attention of older students. In fact, these games are so much fun, students may not even realize they're engaged in vocabulary work! The games here call on students to apply a variety of word-study skills to recognize words and reinforce their meanings. Word Choosy gives you a way to help students master content-specific vocabulary from any subject area, including science, social studies, and math.

CHAPTER 5
GAMES

Word Choosy

Home Run!

Lots of Dots

Word Choosy

In Word Choosy, players answer fill-in-the-blank and True or False questions that test their knowledge of content area vocabulary. Correct answers enable them to travel around the game board as they try to be the first to make it "Home."

VOCABULARY FOCUS Students brush up on challenging content area vocabulary.

Object of This Game

To be the first player to travel around the game board and land on "Home." (Students must answer questions calling on content area vocabulary.)

Number of Players

This game is designed for two to five players, with one student serving as the "reader."

Materials

✔ Word Choosy Game Board (pages 62–63)

✔ Word Choosy Question Cards template (page 64–65)

✔ Die or number cube

✔ Small items to serve as markers, one per player

✔ Cardstock

✔ Heavy paper in two colors

Preparation

1. Photocopy the Word Choosy game board on cardstock and laminate.

2. Photocopy the blank game cards in two different colors.

3. Using one set of colored cards, create the cards in Deck A. On the Deck A cards, write fill-in-the-blank questions based on material students are studying in a particular subject—choose any content area you wish, from math to social studies and science. The questions should come from material students have read. The answer should also be written on the card, so the reader can verify it (see example on the following page).

4. Using another color, create the cards in Deck B. On these cards, write True or False questions based on another subject area, as shown below. Again, write the correct answer at the bottom of the card.

FILL IN THE BLANK	TRUE OR FALSE?
Q: When people have moved from one country to another, we say they have _____ .	**Q:** To find the perimeter of a rectangle, you add the length of all four sides.
A: immigrated	**A:** True

5. In each deck include a few cards that have "Free" written on them. When a player draws a Free card, he or she can use it in a later turn to ignore directions on a space his or her marker lands on.

NOTE

For this game, one student serves as reader. The reader reads the questions and verifies the answers, but does not play.

Directions for Playing

1. Each player selects a marker and rolls the die or number cube to decide the order of play.

2. To leave home base and get on the board, the player must roll a 1.

3. Once on the board, the count on the die or number cube indicates the number of spaces the player moves his or her marker.

- If the marker lands on a space occupied by another player's marker, the two players toss the die. The player who rolls the lower number moves his or her marker back home.

- If the marker lands on a blank space, the marker simply remains on that space and the next player takes a turn.

- If the marker lands on a space with a specific direction, the player follows that direction. If the direction is to choose a card from one of the decks, then the student to the player's right must draw a card for the player and read it to him or her (the player whose turn it is may not see the answer).

    – If a "Free" card is drawn, the reader will hand the card to the player and he or she may use it on a subsequent turn.
    The next player takes a turn.

    – If a question card is drawn and the player answers correctly, he or she may take another turn. If the player answers incorrectly, he or she must stay on the space and answer another question from the same deck on his or her next turn.

4. Play continues until one of the players reaches home and wins the game.

Game Variation

1. The questions on the cards may come from a variety of subject areas rather than just one or two.

2. Have students create question cards.

Word Choosy

Skip a turn

Choose a card from Deck A

START

HOME

Choose a card from Deck B

Place Deck A here.

Take another turn

Skip a turn

Choose a card from Deck A

Choose a card from Deck B

Game Board

Choose a card from Deck B

Move forward 2 spaces

Skip a turn

Choose a card from Deck A

Place Deck B here.

Take another turn

Choose a card from Deck B

Choose a card from Deck A

Move back 4 spaces

Word Choosy Question Cards

TRUE OR FALSE?

Q:

A:

TRUE OR FALSE?

Q:

A:

FREE

TRUE OR FALSE?

Q:

A:

TRUE OR FALSE?

Q:

A:

TRUE OR FALSE?

Q:

A:

Word Choosy Question Cards

FILL IN THE BLANK

Q:

A:

FILL IN THE BLANK

Q:

A:

FREE

FILL IN THE BLANK

Q:

A:

FILL IN THE BLANK

Q:

A:

FILL IN THE BLANK

Q:

A:

Home Run!

Home Run! is based on the rules of baseball, which are familiar to most upper-grade students. As they travel across the three bases of a baseball diamond game board, students gain practice in various vocabulary skills: for example, defining a word or naming an antonym or synonym.

VOCABULARY FOCUS
Students practice a variety of word-study skills to strengthen word ownership.

Object of This Game

To answer specific vocabulary questions to score runs.

Number of Players

This game is designed for two players or teams, with one additional student serving as umpire.

Preparation

1. Photocopy the HomeRun! Diamond Game Board and the Home Run! Scoreboard on cardstock and laminate.

2. Photocopy the blank game cards in on three different colors to create three separate decks of cards.

Materials

✔ Home Run! Diamond Game Board (page 69)

✔ Home Run! Scoreboard (page 70)

✔ Blank Cards template (page 74)

✔ Cardstock

✔ Heavy paper in three colors

✔ Markers (buttons, coin or other small items)—five for each player or team

✔ Water-based pen

NOTE

The set of cards for the first deck (Question cards) will require about 18–24 cards for a complete game. The other decks (Reward and Penalty cards) require only 6–12 cards that can be reused during the game.

3. Using one deck, prepare a set of Question cards containing questions that the player "at bat" must answer. Include the correct answer on the card. The questions should reinforce vocabulary that students are currently studying. Here are some examples of the kinds of questions you might include:

Question Card

Q: Is the word <u>incident</u> an antonym for <u>happening</u>?

A: No. It's a synonym.

- Does a synonym of a word mean the same or opposite of the word?

- Give an antonym for the word *work*.

- What prefix can we use to change the word *fold* to its opposite in meaning?

- Name a suffix that will change the meaning of the verb *excite* to a noun.

4. Using the second deck, prepare the Reward cards, a second set of cards that contain directions the player "at bat" will follow when he or she responds correctly to questions. Directions for these cards might include:

Reward Card

You hit a single. Move to 1st base. Players on base advance one base.

- You hit a single. Advance to 1st base. All players on base advance accordingly

- Error called on opposite team. You take 2nd base. Players on base advance accordingly.

- Double. Take 2nd base—other players move accordingly.

- You hit a home run. All players come home.

5. Using the third deck, prepare the Penalty cards, a third set of cards that penalize the opposite team. In that case the "team" holds the card until the opposing team is "at bat." These cards can be used against an opposing team player. Such cards may read:

Penalty Card

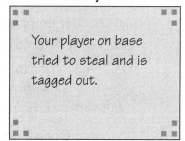

Your player on base tried to steal and is tagged out.

- High fly is caught by the outfielder.

- Player caught off base—called out.

- The ball your opponent hit is called foul.

Directions for Playing

1. Players choose their markers and flip a coin to determine which team is up first.

2. The umpire draws the card on the top of the Question deck and reads it aloud.

3. The player "at bat" responds to the question. If he or she responds correctly, the umpire puts the Question card aside and draws a card from the Reward deck and reads the reward the player receives.

Example:

Umpire: "You hit a single. Take first base and any players on base advance one base."

The player moves his or her marker to the appropriate place on the baseball diamond. In the example above, the player would place a marker on 1st base. The Reward card is then returned to the bottom of the deck and play continues.

NOTE

The umpire uses a water-based pen to keep track of balls, strikes, outs, and runs on the scoreboard.

4. If the player chooses, he or she may request a card from the Penalty deck *instead* of the Reward deck. This card can be used against the opposing team when they are at bat and provide a correct response. The team with the card announces "Penalty," and the team at bat must accept the penalty. The Penalty card is then returned to the bottom of the deck.

5. If the player at bat cannot respond correctly, he or she receives a strike. The umpire returns the Question card to the bottom of the deck and enters the strike on the scorecard. Three outs and the team is retired. The opposing team/player then takes over and the game continues for another inning. The number of innings in the game can vary but should not exceed nine.

6. Scores are based on the number of players to cross home plate.

Game Variation

The teacher may serve as umpire.

Home Run! Diamond
Game Board

2nd
Base

3rd
Base

1st
Base

Home Plate

Home Run! Scoreboard

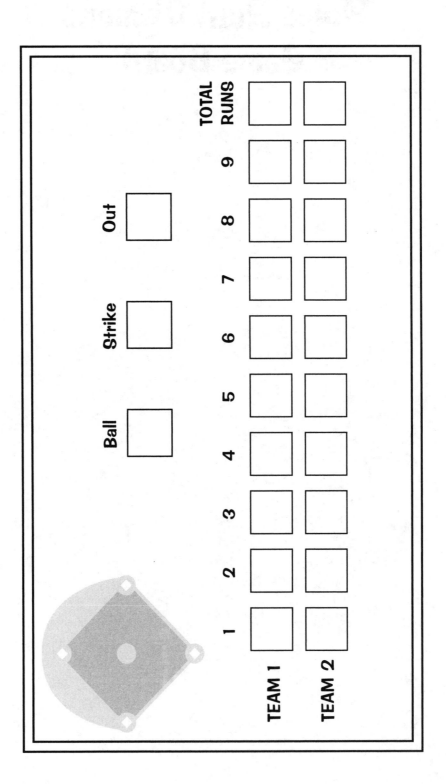

	Ball	Strike	Out

	1	2	3	4	5	6	7	8	9	TOTAL RUNS
TEAM 1										
TEAM 2										

Lots of Dots

Lots of Dots combines a fun strategy game with vocabulary practice as students try to form boxes on the grid and then correctly answer vocabulary questions

VOCABULARY FOCUS

Students will call on a breadth of word-study skills as they reinforce word knowledge.

Object of This Game

To claim the most boxes on the grid. (Players connect dots to complete the box, then claim it by correctly answering a vocabulary question.)

Number of Players

This game is designed for two to four players, with an additional student to serve as monitor.

Materials

✔ Lots of Dots Grid (page 73)

✔ Blank Cards template (page 74)

✔ Colored pencils (different color for each player)

✔ Die or number cube

✔ Cardstock and water-based pens (optional)

Preparation

1. Photocopy the Lots of Dots Grid and the word card template. (Use cardstock for the grid if you wish to laminate it for repeated use with water-based pens.)

2. Make a list of at least 25 vocabulary words that you'd like students to practice. The game requires students to employ a variety of vocabulary skills, such as thinking of synonyms, antonyms, and using the target word in an imaginary newspaper headline.

Directions for Playing

1. Give each player a different-colored pencil. Order of play is decided by flipping a coin.

2. The first player begins by connecting two dots.

3. The next players take a turn, and play continues, with each player connecting two dots. The object is to be the one to *complete* a box by drawing the fourth side.

NOTE

This game relies on strategy. You may need to help younger students understand that the object is to complete the box. They should avoid (if they can!) drawing the third side of a box, as this will give opponents the opportunity to finish the box and claim it.

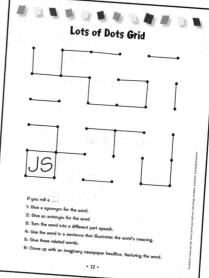

4. When the player completes a box, the monitor draws a card and reads it.

5. The player who completed the box rolls the die or number cube. Then, depending on the number rolled, he or she follows the direction listed beneath the grid.

6. If other players agree that he or she has supplied the correct answer or example, the player claims the box by putting his or her initials in the box and play continues.

7. If the players agree that the answer given is not sufficient, the player whose turn is next can roll the die and follow step 5 in an attempt to claim the box.

8. In case of disputes, the monitor is responsible for determining if the answer is acceptable.

9. The player with the most boxes is the winner.

Game Variation

Have students select vocabulary words and create the word cards.

Lots of Dots Grid

If you roll a . . .

1: Give a synonym for the word.

2: Give an antonym for the word

3: Turn the word into a different part speech.

4: Use the word in a sentence that illustrates the word's meaning.

5: Give three related words.

6: Come up with an imaginary newspaper headline, featuring the word.

Blank Cards

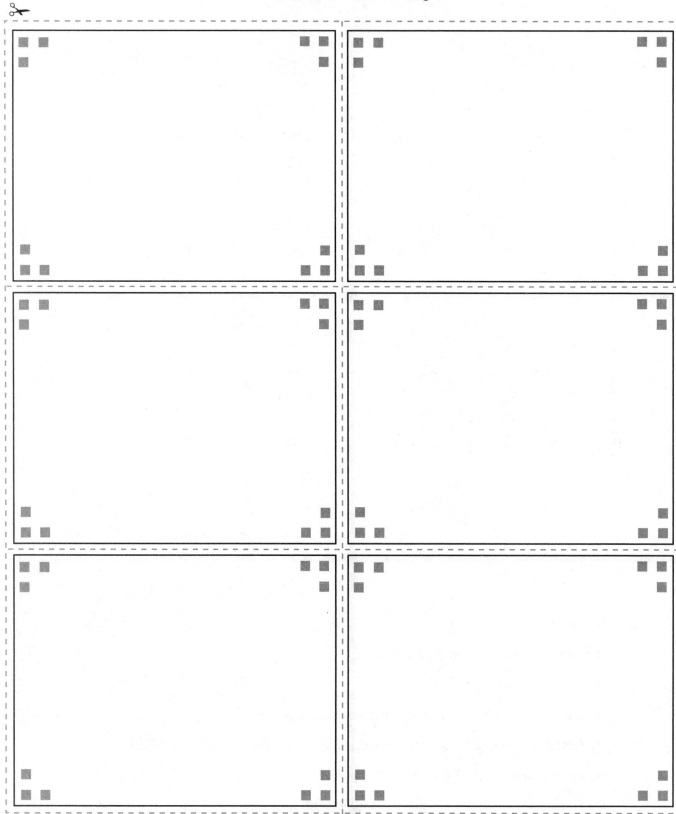

Appendix

Antonyms

above/below	boring/exciting	effect/cause	from/to
absent/present	bottom/top	easy/difficult	front/back
achieve/fail	boy/girl	empty/full	frozen/melted
add/subtract	break/fix	ending/beginning	girl/boy
admire/dislike	bright/dim	enemy/friend	give/take
admit/reject	buy/sell	enjoy/hate	go/stop
adult/child	cause/effect	enter/exit	good/bad
afraid/confident	cheap/expensive	even/odd	guilty/innocent
against/for	clean/dirty	evening/morning	happy/sad
alive/dead	cold/hot	evil/good	hard/soft
all/none	come/go	exciting/boring	harm/help
allow/forbid	cooked/raw	fact/fiction	hate/love
alone/together	cool/warm	fail/pass	heal/hurt
always/never	coward/hero	false/true	hear/ignore
ancient/modern	cruel/kind	fancy/plain	heavy/light
answer/question	cry/laugh	far/near	high/low
appear/vanish	curved/straight	fast/slow	hot/cold
arrive/depart	dangerous/safe	fat/thin	imaginary/real
ask/tell	dark/light	female/male	improve/damage
asked/told	day/night	few/many	icy/warm
asleep/awake	deep/shallow	fiction/fact	ill/healthy
attack/defend	defend/attack	find/lose	illegal/legal
back/front	different/same	finish/start	in/out
backward/forward	dim/bright	first/last	increase/decrease
beautiful/ugly	dirty/clean	flexible/rigid	inside/outside
before/after	dry/wet	float/sink	joy/grief
beginning/end	dull/bright	follow/lead	kind/cruel
big/little	dwarf/giant	foolish/wise	large/small
birth/death	eager/lazy	for/against	last/first
black/white	early/late	forget/remember	late/early
blame/forgive	earn/spend	forward/backward	laugh/cry
blunt/sharp	east/west	friend/stranger	lead/follow

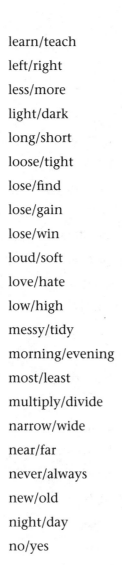

learn/teach	noisy/quiet	remain/change	sunrise/sunset
left/right	north/south	repair/break	start/finish
less/more	nothing/everything	rich/poor	stop/start
light/dark	obey/command	right/wrong	sweet/sour
long/short	odd/even	rough/smooth	tall/short
loose/tight	often/seldom	rude/polite	tame/wild
lose/find	old/young	sad/funny	thick/thin
lose/gain	on/off	sad/glad	to/from
lose/win	open/close	safe/dangerous	top/bottom
loud/soft	over/under	same/different	true/false
love/hate	pain/joy	shallow/deep	ugly/pretty
low/high	pass/fail	short/long	under/over
messy/tidy	plain/fancy	shout/whisper	up/down
morning/evening	pleasure/pain	shut/open	white/black
most/least	poor/rich	silly/serious	whole/part
multiply/divide	present/absent	simple/complex	with/without
narrow/wide	private/public	sit/stand	work/play
near/far	push/pull	slow/fast	yes/no
never/always	question/answer	small/large	young/old
new/old	quick/slow	smooth/rough	
night/day	raise/lower	soft/hard	
no/yes	real/imaginary	spend/earn	

Synonyms

add/total	before/prior	dangerous/hazard-	end/finish
after/following	begin/start	ous	enough/sufficient
all/every	below/under	decrease/lessen	error/mistake
anger/rage	bitter/tart	delay/postpone	fat/chubby
appear/look	brave/courageous	demonstrate/show	fetch/get
appreciative/thank-	call/yell	different/diverse	find/locate
ful	car/vehicle	dislike/detest	fix/mend
arrive/reach	change/swap	divide/split	forgive/excuse
ask/question	city/town	during/while	fortune/wealth
baby/infant	close/shut	earth/world	fragile/delicate
back/rear	continue/persist	eat/consume	freedom/liberty

frequent/often

giant/huge

gift/present

give/donate

grab/take

grow/develop

guide/lead

happy/glad

hasten/hurry

heal/cure

high/tall

hold/grasp

huge/vast

idea/concept

illegal/wrong

income/earnings

injure/hurt

insult/offend

job/occupation

jump/leap

just/fair

keep/save

kind/considerate

large/big

last/persist

late/tardy

leave/depart

like/enjoy

listen/hear

little/small

make/build

mark/label

mean/cruel

messy/sloppy

mend/repair

mistake/error

model/example

move/transport

naughty/bad

near/close

neat/tidy

need/require

new/fresh

obey/follow

odor/smell

often/frequently

omit/delete

operate/use

overdue/late

own/have

pack/fill

pain/ache

pair/couple

part/piece

peak/summit

perform/act

pick/choose

praise/applaud

quaint/odd

quake/shake

quick/fast

quiet/silent

quit/stop

quiz/test

rage/fury

rain/shower

raise/increase

record/write

relax/rest

repeat/echo

revise/change

rule/law

safe/secure

say/tell

scrape/scratch

scream/shout

sharp/pointed

shove/push

splash/spray

spring/bounce

sour/tart

tear/rip

terrify/scare

thin/slender

tiny/small

touch/feel

trail/path

try/attempt

tug/pull

understand/know

undo/untie

unstable/wobbly

untamed/wild

untidy/messy

uproar/noise

use/apply

usual/common

utter/talk

slam/bang

vacant/empty

vacation/break

value/worth

vanish/disappear

vary/change

violent/rough

vital/necessary

wag/wave

wail/cry

walk/stroll

warn/alert

wash/clean

well/healthy

whack/hit

whole/entire

yank/pull

yell/shout

yummy/tasty

zilch/nothing

zoom/rush

Prefixes & Suffixes

-er (comparative)

bigger	fuller	madder	sicker
brighter	funnier	meaner	slower
busier	happier	narrower	smaller
cleaner	higher	nearer	smoother
clearer	hotter	nicer	softer
colder	kinder	older	sooner
darker	larger	poorer	straighter
deeper	lesser	prettier	taller
earlier	lighter	quicker	thicker
fairer	littler	rounder	warmer
faster	longer	sadder	wider
fewer	louder	safer	
fresher	lower	shorter	

-est (superlative)

biggest	fullest	meanest	slowest
brightest	funniest	narrowest	smallest
busiest	happiest	nearest	smoothest
cleanest	healthiest	nicest	softest
clearest	highest	oldest	soonest
coldest	hottest	poorest	stillest
darkest	kindest	prettiest	straightest
deepest	largest	quickest	tallest
earliest	lightest	roundest	thickest
fairest	longest	saddest	warmest
fastest	loudest	softest	widest
fewest	lowest	shortest	
freshest	maddest	sickest	

-ful

armful	forceful	mouthful	tankful
beautiful	forgetful	painful	tasteful
bowlful	frightful	peaceful	thankful
careful	graceful	playful	thoughtful
cheerful	handful	restful	truthful
colorful	healthful	roomful	useful
cupful	helpful	skillful	willful
doubtful	hopeful	spoonful	wonderful
fearful	joyful	successful	

in-, im-, ir-, il-

illegal	impetuous	incomplete	ingrown
illegible	impolite	inconvenient	injustice
illiterate	impossible	incorrect	insane
imbalance	impractical	indefinite	insatiable
immaterial	improper	indignant	inseparable
immature	impure	indirect	insight
immodest	inaccurate	indistinct	invaluable
immortal	inadequate	indoors	invisible
immovable	inappropriate	inefficient	irrational
impartial	inboard	inevitable	irregular
impassable	inbounds	inexpensive	irresistible
impatient	incapable	inexperienced	irresponsible
imperfect	incase	infinite	irrevocably
impersonal	incompetent	infrequent	

References

Allen, J. (1999) *Words, Words, Words: Teaching Vocabulary in Grades 4-12*. York, Maine: Stenhouse.

Balchowicz, C., Fisher, P., & Ogle, D. (2006) Vocabulary: Questions from the Classroom. *Reading Research Quarterly, 41, 4,* 524–539.

Beal, G. (1991) *Kingfisher's Book of Words*. New York: Kingfisher.

Beck, I., McKeown, M. & Kucan, L. (2002) *Bringing Words to Life*. New York: Guilford.

Blevins, W. (2001).*Teaching Phonics & Word Study in the Intermediate Grades: A Complete Source Book*. New York: Scholastic.

Carroll, J. B., Davies, P. & Richman, B. (1971) *Word Frequency Book*. Boston: Houghton Mifflin.

Clark, J. O. E. 1988. *Word for Word: A Dictionary of Synonyms*. New York: Henry Holt.

Funk, C. E. (1993) 2107 *Curious Word Origins, Sayings and Expressions*. New York: Galahad.

Iggulden, G. & Iggulden, H. 2007. *The Dangerous Book for Boys*. NY: HarperCollins.

Johnson, D. (2001) *Vocabulary in the Elementary and Middle School*. Boston: Allyn & Bacon.

Ryder, R. J. & Slater, W. H. (1988). The Relationship Between Word Frequency and Word Knowledge. *Journal of Educational Research, 81,* 312–317.